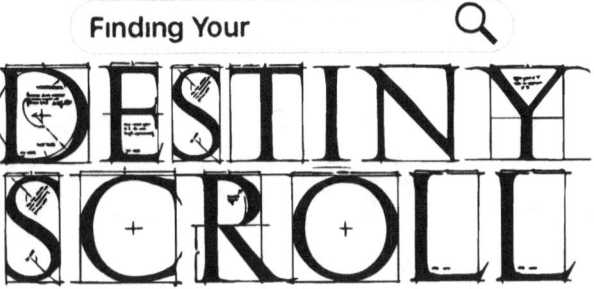

Finding Your DESTINY SCROLL

by

SHERI SCOTT

Illustrations by

Karalyn Kohan

FINDING YOUR DESTINY SCROLL
Copyright ©2019 by Sheri Scott.
Illustrations copyright ©2019 by Karalyn Kohan
Book design by lukacsmedia
All rights reserved.

No part of this book may be used or reproduced
in any manner whatsoever, or stored in a retrieval system,
or transmitted in any form or by any means, electronic, mechanical,
photocopying or otherwise, without written permission
except in the case of brief quotations embodied
in critical articles and reviews.
For information address:

Published by: SHAREALIKE
An Imprint of SHARE *Publishing*
A division of Share Resources Inc.
Calgary, Alberta, Canada.
www.shareresourcesinc.com

ISBN 978-1-989269-18-3 (paperback)
First Edition

Dedication

This book is dedicated to all those who have participated in the Messenger discussion groups I was a part of. All of your questions, interest, sharing and listening ears have helped me frame some of my experiences in heavenly realms. Everything I have put in writing has assisted me on my journey into my Father's house.

Special Thanks

I would like to express my gratitude to Karalyn Kohan for the illustrations contained in this book. One day a window opened and I saw illustrations speckled throughout the pages and presented her with the idea of creating some drawings. She graciously accepted the invitation to draw what she saw as she engaged with this endeavor.

Introduction

I am affectionately calling this - the book that wrote itself. When I realized I had written a fair amount of information, while sharing in this Messenger discussion group, I decided to compile my posts into a chronicle of sharing. There is repetition in my answers as new people would join the discussion and ask similar questions. I have left these as they appeared because I found even my own repeated sharing has helped me frame my experiences. In some instances, I am answering a question I no longer remember and it seems like a disjointed statement. I have left these in their context because they caused me to wonder anew and I am hoping they cause you to wonder as well!

Somewhere along the way we added the topic of mountains to the scroll discussion so some of that is included as well. Posts from the Business Discussion group have also been included on the same dates as it helps to maintain and contextualize some of the flow I was in on that date or timeframe as it pertained to my destiny scroll.

When editing to complete my sentences and expand my shorthand, I have realized that many statements begin with 'I'. This is because my sharing is personally about me or my understanding. From a writing standpoint, this would be a silly way to intentionally write a book, but again, this book wrote itself and I chose to leave it that way. In order that it would be obvious this is a one-sided conversation, I wanted to format the text in word bubbles all on one side of the page, but I'll just tell you this is only my side of the chat.

This Messenger discussion group was formed by Jane Johnson, founder of One United Body (formerly Ecclesia Framework), and I was honoured to loosely facilitate conversation for a stretch of time. Jane has been relentless in her pursuit of her role in heavenly realms as a son of God and joint heir with Yeshua. She has created an online environment for others to begin accessing heaven and accelerate in maturing. One of my favorite blessings I received from Jane is her commitment to relationship. It is with honor and delight that I share my participation. www.oneunitedbody.org

All scripture is either a loose paraphrase, or quoted to the best of my ability as this was a conversation.

December 6 - The First Post

I presented myself as a living sacrifice to Jesus to open my scroll (written on my heart). Then I had an encounter where Jesus took me into a library and showed me a large book that was open on a table. I knew it was mine. When I asked him what it was, he responded with, "this is the page you are on". It had writing on the page that I couldn't read as it seemed like another language.

Each page in the book seems to be for a few months at a time. When I think of asking to see my book, I ask Jesus to see more and then we go to the book in the library and turn a page. I think I am prompted to ask when it is time to see what is next because I am not always thinking about my book.

One time we turned a page and there was a full-page picture. As soon as I began to ask about it, I went right inside the picture. When I was done what I was supposed to do in the picture, I came back out and was in the library again. The last page was four months ago - I have been working on one page that long. Most pages seem to contain some concepts as well as specifics.

For example, one page had three pillars on it. I set my desire to be a pillar and to understand what the function of a pillar is, and then I was also invested in a bench of three. The pillars on the page were tiered and I couldn't seem to grasp why, so I kept engaging with this page.

When I asked if I could see the next page, Jesus showed it to me. Around this time, I heard about nine pillars

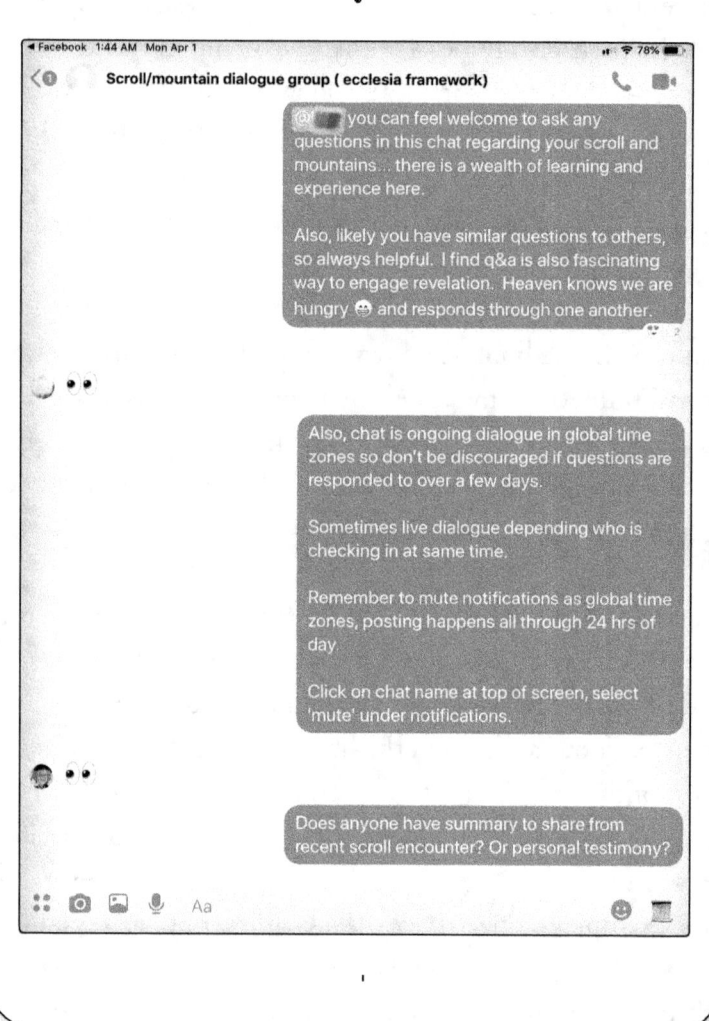

of ascension mentioned for the first time in a conference and knew that was why the pillars on my page were tiered.

I felt a particular business was on my scroll but I wasn't certain so I asked Jesus to see it in the future to know if it exists there. He showed me two things on my scroll in the future that confirmed this for me, one was the logo for my business and the other was completed books available for sale in a bookstore. Authoring is also on my scroll. My logo was different than I had been currently working on with a designer. The logo was blueprint blue and I would have never picked that as a color, yet I promptly changed my logo.

I just asked to see my scroll although I had heard of people going to a scroll room and I hadn't been there before today. I also heard someone say that our miscarried, aborted and deceased children in heaven are waiting for someone in their bloodline to release their destiny scrolls so they can move forward in their heavenly inheritance as well.

I decided to ask Jesus if I could release my deceased son's scroll. We met together and the three of us went into this pulsating scroll room. Jesus handed me my son's scroll, I handed it to my son, and the three of us immediately became one being. It was really powerful.

I can't remember what happened after that, although I had the sense that my son will be functioning as an advisor for me. My son had told me long ago before I knew who he was, or that he was my son, that he would back me or invest in me. He is really matured in heaven.

As for daily mandates or day to day scroll out-working, I sense this and move in it more intuitively. I can feel the ease of doing what I am supposed to do and the lack of peace, or disharmony when not doing what I am supposed to. It is getting easier day by day to discern the flow. I would like to incorporate a daily protocol of checking in with my scroll and with the Trinity, before I am fully in the middle of my day. Often, I am busy before I realize the day is half gone. Sometimes I carry on in the day from whatever was going on in the night as if I wake up already in a flow of sorts.

One time I ended up trading all my dreams, hopes and desires and it was so ridiculously painful. I had to do it more than once as I think I kept holding on to just a little of my dreams not knowing what might fill the void if I gave them up entirely. I really only wanted what he wants, no matter how wonderful my plans were to me!

December 11

Redemptive gifts from Romans 12: I haven't seen myself functioning in all of them strongly yet I know for the time being I am strongly wired as prophet = vision and design, it is the easiest way I process information and revelation. I am always seeing structure, how things work, evaluating efficacy, innovating new paradigms. My life so far has been on the front side of emerging technologies, emerging industries, paradigm shifts, including my own spiritual growth. I am always looking for what isn't there yet in the body of Christ, the earth, the plan, the big picture and the drive is so deep.

I think we will balance out in all of the Romans 12 redemptive gifts as we are being made like Jesus, yet I am still working with where I am at currently even though I see more available and desire that.

December 12

As for my scroll, I have authoring, inventions, technology and business categorically and my drive in all these areas is to produce and reproduce. I desire to help others in these areas, to help people do these things on their scrolls and learning how to function in creating, seeding, reproducing in the business arena. I love sharing.

Also, I have a desire in framing heavenly structures on earth, models, governmental structures, new realities. I don't even think this desire is for now so much, I think the framing is for those to come. I expect our function in heavenly realms is so much broader than the remainder of this time & space portion.

December 13

I did notice somewhere I read something about asking your Father to imprint on your heart and I want to say that I believe our scroll is already imprinted or written on our hearts.

The fast facilitation of accessing your destiny scroll is to ask the Lion of the Tribe of Judah - the one who is worthy to open the scroll, to open your scroll. This is essentially presenting yourself as a living sacrifice to the high priest, Jesus, who opens your scroll.

This living sacrifice also opens or clears our first love gate and invites the Trinity into our being to begin to will to do his will.

December 18

I think in a priestly function we can act on others' behalf that are unbelievers as we will see things in order to deal with that. We wouldn't necessarily share anything with them unless we are told to. Holy Spirit is awesome in the delicate dance with unbelievers.

We can also ask to see a person's scroll and then tell some of it to them. This is what I think every prophetic word should be like. Be aware you may not be able to see anyone else's scroll.

Our scrolls are written on our hearts so you can start by presenting yourself to Jesus as your high priest as a living sacrifice, he is the one worthy to open scrolls.

December 19

I have had an encounter with Wisdom where she told me things to tell a couple friends. These are people who can and do access heaven themselves and also have met Wisdom. It was a one off and it hasn't happened again, so far.

The previous reference to reading someone's scroll to them was in response to evangelism comments regarding unbelievers. The pages in my book that I have seen contain words in a language that isn't English and sometimes full-page pictures.

Sometimes there are pictures as if they were words. I have been sorting through the last page I was shown, searching it out.

I now realize it is a picture of pillars of ascension which I know nothing about. I have a sense that they are connected to New Jerusalem, a wheel within a wheel, twelve pillars under a mountain and operating in dimensions within a realm.

Understanding most of these things has been so large to grasp for me.

I have listened to some podcasts and teachings repeatedly and I go over and over them about building an altar, being a living sacrifice, how the seventy in the book of Genesis went into heaven with their bodies, how the sun is a gate, there are kings from other realms, we are the gate into this realm and other fun stuff plus building an altar under a mountain.

Now that I have encountered more in heavenly realms, some of the things I have heard described make a bit more sense.

December 20
Yes, I am hungry for sure as I am progressing through these heavenly realms adventures. I have recently been seeing a full priest's ephod on me every time I consciously dial in.

It is an ephod with urim and thummim and provides access to four ages although I don't fully comprehend that. It's so chewy, but I love the structure.

December 21
I came to a resolve at some point that if I chose to pull out of the busyness of doing anything (church included) for one year to actually focus on my relationship with my Father and enter his rest, ceasing from my striving- that would be an incredibly valuable year of my life.

It changed my perspective and took that invisible pressure off to perform, or grow, or be something, or do something fruitful. I am way more chill now than ever in my life.

December 22
Daily mandates - what do you do daily to determine the flow of your day?

I have one friend who starts every morning with the counsel of the Trinity to get a scroll for the day. It is specific. I see some things as running threads through my life and when I'm in rest, things line up according to purpose or mandate. I seem to function intuitively in the day to day things and can usually tell when I am off track because my peace leaves. Staying checked in, or engaged really helps. When do you notice you are 'in the groove' or flow? Where there is joy and ease. Some people wake up in the morning with mandates coming out of their spirit.

December 27
Regarding redemptive gifts, I think the word 'gifts' throws people off as it isn't an additional endowment,

such as 'gifts of the Holy Spirit'. Romans 12 identifies functions and maturity within that wiring. It identifies how we perceive and what we value.

I have always thought and functioned like a prophet gift, it happens in how I process information, I track patterns and principles and design and structure and put them together to 'see'. It is a grace afforded me to fulfill my destiny.

The Romans 12 scripture says, for just as each of us has one body with many members, and these members do not all have the same function, so in Christ we, though many, form one body, and each member belongs to all the others. We have different gifts, according to the grace given to each of us. If your gift is prophesying, then prophesy in accordance with your faith; if it is serving, then serve; if it is teaching, then teach; if it is to encourage, then give encouragement; if it is giving, then give generously; if it is to lead, do it diligently; if it is to show mercy, do it cheerfully.

I think that there would be seven approaches to legislation, seven perspectives as an oracle, seven interpretations of a priest, seven motivations of a king.

As for spiritual gifts or supernatural endowments such as healing, tongues, prophecy, miracles etc., I believe these serve a purpose and likely in a far greater measure than we currently know. I think we should all be a natural flow of these gifts, having all available to give at any time. Many have never functioned in these gifts or received from them.

...names are written in the Lamb's book of life.
Revelation 21: 27

The giving of apostles, prophets, teachers, evangelists, pastors (or five-fold ministry) was for maturing the body until we grow up into the head, Jesus.

I have heard it identified as the five-fold ministry being the government of the kingdom age. Most of us (in this discussion) should be living out of higher age than this so the five-fold ministry is no longer what governs or teaches us as we are being taught by the Lord. It has been taught that there are five that govern each age in the earth, but I don't have the experience of what five for what age.

I don't consider Romans 12 redemptive gifts to actually be gifts, they are graces given by God to accomplish our destiny - so they work with our scroll not instead of a scroll.

About operating out of strengths or gifts - I think language is not serving us with the word 'gifts'. I agree also that it is easy to rely on our own strength if we are gifted in an area, rather than dependency on our Father and our heavenly family to fulfill our scroll. Aha! Romans 12… Seven interfaces. How we interface with each other and earth realm and heaven? I think also that the seven interfaces line up with the seven spirits of God. I have thought that for a long time yet haven't 'seen' it.

December 28

As part of having the ecclesia on our destiny scrolls and knowing we are to love the body, whoever feels led to help remove obstacles on the highway of holiness from the way of God's people, on behalf of existing ministries - this would benefit the wider body.

January 3

Sometimes I think we 'believe' things are more elusive than they really are. Like for example, we can ask Jesus to see our scroll yet we wait for him to show it to us. I am not sure what makes the shift in our minds but, things accelerate when we realize he's waiting for us. No condemnation or pressure because when we are ready, we pursue.

Side note, if you have a business, your business will have a mountain. I have heard it mentioned that if you aren't governing your business mountain, something else will be, so that's a good place to start.

January 9

Daily mandates:

I tend to function intuitively in daily mandates. I 'feel' like I should go here and not there, and something comes of it. I call a person today and not tomorrow because I get an urgency. Mostly it feels like a flow from rest where things happen, opportunities show up, problems get solved and I do what needs to be done.

Lately I have really relaxed into the idea that from rest, I will know what, when and who I am to interact with in my day to day life, in this realm and in heavenly realms.

This also ties into 'seasons' and 'purposes', for example, in this season I am not taking on any extra responsibilities beyond what I have already. So, this means I am not leading anything, not administrating anything, not coordinating anything, and much of what I am doing is coordinated, lead and administered by others. This is a season, as I have other seasons, where I initiate action and activity in almost every area of my life!

Purposes to me are more like objectives rather than mandates, but it might be a language distinction only. For example, I feel a desire to help connect the people pursuing heavenly realms in my city. I felt to begin hosting a meetup once a month in a coffee shop. I am not leading, I am only facilitating connections. It is not mandatory and I sense there is a higher purpose to connections being made than I can see now. I'm being obedient and I know it is temporary until meetups have fulfilled their purpose.

My experience of this flow is simply walking in the spirit which is something I think we all do in our relationship with the Trinity. Unlocking my scroll of destiny reveals bigger purposes unto which the day to day leads to.

It also includes heavenly purposes which I didn't know I had before. My sons are enrolled in a dual credit program and are doing high school and post-secondary at the same time and their course credits count for both. Likewise, I have dual destiny.

A Scroll for a Mandate:

You will get scrolls or create them, as you are engaging in heavenly realms. You will know what to do with them as you will be in an encounter, if you are unsure you can ask Jesus, or whoever you are with.

January 14

I have found a cycle in growing and maturing. I spend time with Jesus and the Father and Holy Spirit and they show me stuff. The new revelation uncovers my junk (things I am bound or governed by or struggle with). I go get my newly uncovered sin and iniquity in my DNA judged. Then I can see and understand more and my view broadens. Then they show me more and the new revelation uncovers more of my junk, I go get judged and the cycle continues.

I get anything that doesn't look like Jesus judged under his blood and it increases my ability to see and understand and so on and so on. It feels a bit like tacking in a sailboat. There are parts of my scroll that don't get revealed to me until I am ready to move forward. The path is very cleverly orchestrated.

January 15

I saw my business mountain as I formulated a business plan. I also went into the future and saw the logo and then it took quite a while to realize the mountain was the logo, it is a cube. I have a ministry type mountain that came into view as I was able to see. I had been engaging inside it in a counsel room and didn't realize it was the inside of the mountain. Sometimes I find it funny how obvious some things become in hindsight. Currently I am governing other areas of my life from my personal mountain. I have found multi-function there. Lately I have been trying to engage the mountain for my city. I have had several encounters mandating angels and engaging the church angels in the city, but have yet to see the mountain.

January 16

I'm not sure why scrolls or books look different for different people yet we have more than one scroll or book. One is a book of record, one is a book of destiny. I have only seen my destiny book so far, but I know I also have a book of personal revelations that were written with tears through the years. I have a book of record that is sometimes read in a courtroom scenario although, I have only seen blank pages.

What I saw in the library was my book of destiny and I only see the bit in front of me, like seasons and they are not super detailed. Daily scrolls, or mandates, help with more details and specifics. You can ask Jesus, Father and Holy Spirit to see more at any time.

Your eyes saw my unformed body; all the days ordained for me were written in your book before one of them came to be.

Psalm 139:16

January 18

The simplicity of it all is, us in him and him in us, and it all stems from there. We don't need to know it all or see and understand it all, we need to abide, rest and enjoy him. I am seeing the ebb and flow of complexity, simplicity, complexity, simplicity and on.

January 26

I am curious if any of you with an interest, or you feel a pull towards the Martial Arts, have untethered from Mars? We are governed and tethered to planets and stars by frequencies, they are connected in our neural networks in our brain and imprinted on the waters in our cells. If any have testimony of this I would love to hear it.

What is untether? Well, that's a lot to answer. Untether is to sever an existing connection. You can ask Jesus to show you other governments over your bloodline in your DNA and then you essentially want to untether from those governing entities, and reposition or tether yourself to government of Father, Son and Holy Spirit. Much like being untangled from a web.

You'll need to sort out where you think the new age line is to your own understanding and then ask Jesus. Some current understanding sounds like we go so far as mystics and then it crosses a line and becomes new age, in a linear manner.

My current understanding is that both are happening in different realms at the same time and much of it is the same.

Witches and warlocks trade on stars, have corrupted them and those in new age are advancing an agenda in the planets, stars and galaxies AND so are the sons of God. I'm focused on having my Father teach me how to govern his kingdom and creation.

I plead guilty in court for my (bloodline) having traded with whatever entity to gain power, position, provision or protection. I get that judged and then petition for severing contracts, ties and connections, then I state my intention and actively reposition under the government of the kingdom of my Father. Usually a handful of scriptures come to mind as the basis for my petition.

January 28

I think there is a balance with regard to newer people. Our part is to encourage one another and share our experiences and their intimacy and growth is between them and Jesus, Father and Holy Spirit. Sensitivity is required with newer people as we all know how many questions come from one bit of revelation. Also, we need to be conscious of the intents of our heart and specifically not being motivated by false responsibility or self-exaltation, we need love as our motivation.

For those interested in knowing your scroll, there are teachings available on the Internet for presenting yourself as a living sacrifice to Jesus. Your scroll is written on your heart and Jesus is worthy to open it, this is a great start point.

Now, some jump right in and ask to go to the scroll room and ask to see their scroll, and this happens too. We are all coming into heavenly realms at different levels of maturity and intimacy and responsibility so our process may look different from other people's. I haven't been to a scroll room as others describe. I went to a large library with my book on a table and Jesus showed me the page I am on and angels assigned to me were there also. We discuss the page together.

Each page in my book is a season, usually a few months at a time and the daily dealings are more intuitive as I am led. The scriptural idea of dying to ourselves, or not loving our lives unto death, is exactly why presenting ourselves as a living sacrifice is required. Along with this is opening our first love gate to allow him in to work. My next step was to find the seat of rest and cease from my own striving.

January 31
I have had a few encounters that involved the earth and heavens passing away and new heavens and new earth being created. It seemed like a tidy blip rather than cataclysmic. Maybe because I saw it from another realm? Not this one?

February 8
You can petition in court for untethering and then tether to heaven, to the Trinity, or you can state that you are untethering from your mountain. You can entangle in light with the Trinity as well.

February 13

Part of maturity we are being led into is knowing how to govern. There is a grace for the heart of the intercessor, and I believe they will rise up in governance with a level of understanding mandates that many in body of Christ currently grasp for.

I personally only seek out areas of need that I am called to clearly, as there are many in the body who are called to different arenas or spheres of influence. This is why it is important to know what is on your scroll, so you are not distracted by things you aren't supposed to be doing no matter how well meaning they are. As we move more into following our destiny (which is important regardless of appearance) we become satisfied when we fulfill it. Which could be to act or not act on a particular request.

February 25

I was thinking about seeing and knowing your scroll and I think this is the foundation that comes from our relationship with our Father, Jesus and Holy Spirit. It is our destiny that we outwork together with them.

One of the first steps I found was presenting myself as a living sacrifice. I listened to a teaching on this and essentially it says to present yourself to Jesus as your high priest, who is worthy to open the scroll on your heart. There are books and scrolls to look at as well and I am not sure why some people see scrolls and some see books. There is book of life or book of record and book of destiny. I suspect there are more as I have a book of revelations that angels have created for me.

I have encountered picture portals where you go right inside a picture in a book and end up somewhere else. You can ask to be shown your scroll and become acquainted with relationally accessing it.

Often staying aligned with your scroll becomes intuitive on a day to day basis. You will notice obvious things that are not on your scroll by the level of effort or level of peace associated with them. I have heard many refer to a scroll room. I have seen a few places for scroll storage yet my book is in a huge library, with tables from one end to the other. Usually my angels are with me and Jesus as we discuss what is on each page. Pages seem to be short seasons of three months or six months.

I am usually led to ask to see next page and it usually requires a foundation from previous page of revelation, understanding and maturity. I have not seen a daily version of this, although it is written on my heart so I expect to simply know.

I regularly focus on having entered into and living from his rest so I am not striving for destiny. I am not looking for a plan or direction so I can be told or shown what to do. I believe there is a correlation between willingness to be responsible for our destiny and the clarity, pace and outworking of it. I believe we accelerate by desire and maturing.

February 25

I saw how our Father gifted craftsman and metal workers etc. to build the temple, for each to do what was needed with a supernatural endowment. This is a unity of purpose unto a bigger picture and it is for the king and his kingdom.

I got this too, Jeremiah 29:7
"Also, seek the peace and prosperity of the city to which I have carried you into exile. Pray to the LORD for it, because if it prospers, you too will prosper."
I saw the earth is our exile city and not our home but, seek peace and prosperity for it.

In the business encounter, the crystal floor we saw was by where the pillars were. I felt the individual connection to the blueprint was because each thing resembles something we already carried in our heart. And this was the opportunity to release the blueprint into the earth. I have never seen or done anything like that so am only going on my best sense at the time.

I will be taking it into court of war or strategy to explore it further with Jesus. I am curious what the personal implications are or might be, if any at all. The blueprint I saw was for judging unjust scales, a level of corruption.

February 28

I have noticed that same deceptive thought regarding the idea that you have no authority if you are not victorious yourself. Although there is an increasing understanding of authority, and we are blind in certain areas, all of our authority is in his name so it doesn't seem to matter what state you are in. Truth is where our authority comes from and it is Jesus - I have told liars and thoughts (that I must have victory in order to have authority), to back off as I position in his authority.

March 2

I have been noticing lots of shifting priorities for people, not just in these chat groups (people coming and going), but in general. I felt it last week and it feels like things are changing and adjusting very quickly in my life. Is anyone else feeling a stir? I'm not sure how to describe it, yet it is the same thing others are describing. I experience some intense uncovering and then a feeling of peaceful release. I feel a certainty or confidence that literally just showed up.

March 7

I think as we are more consciously aware of our place in heaven, our oneness with him and the reality of that, we begin to 'function' as him, in all realms. Much different than the relationally distant way of reading about him and then trying to be like that. The difference between emulating him and being one with him.

March 7

So, I have been intrigued by global finance although I have no background in this nor have I researched much. I ran across 'star trading' regarding a method for day trading in stock and currency markets. Apparently, someone has tracked the astrological patterns of movement and correlations of how markets move on earth in specific timing. This affects global economies and global trade which then in turn affects the business climate nationally, regionally and locally.

I believe we are to govern star houses and their effect on the earth, and then as an outflow, global finance as one aspect of that. Some people in heavenly realms communities are understanding and participating in this, although not much revelation is shared, or teaching on it. There is much more teaching in the new age camp and although it is higher knowledge, it is from the wrong kingdom.

I get the sense that the blueprints we released in the business discussion group were a higher authority and were from above the star houses so had to pass through them when imprinted into earth. I don't know how to explain that other than like an overlay.

I have a couple of ideas regarding finance, one idea is a kingdom crowdfunding company. What I am seeing is a method to move finances globally within a closed system. Although it would be governed by international finance laws, it would be a framework to move money within a global body.

> Gofundme has moved over $3B in the first 6 years.
> Kickstarter has moved $2.8B in the first 4.5 years.
> Indiegogo has smaller numbers but it is only arts related at $800M in its first 7 years.

I am releasing my desire to see a Kingdom of God version of this type of money transfer system. Woohoo. I feel it's a pathway or framework that in the outset, would look like any other crowdfunding platform but would be a method or system to transact fast movement of finances as the Lord needs. Similar to the idea of going into a town and finding a donkey and appropriating it for his use. This could also function as a venture capital fund I think, outside of traditional large volume transfers, it would be in smaller increments. Like a storehouse managed by a Joseph, but for our Father rather than Pharaoh, in this realm.

I can't honestly grasp the implications of a closed money system but needed to release that. I don't believe that is on my scroll yet felt releasing it, was.

March 12

I just recently had an encounter where I moved beyond my understanding. I was told in court of judges, that they would rule in favor of anything written on my scroll, whether I understood it or not. It felt like a safeguard where I could proceed with things even without the clarity of 'exactly' what was going on. I asked the bench in angels court the same thing and Jesus told me I could release any mandate I was given and that my agreement mattered.

I already agree with the purposes of heaven because of my heart, so even without understanding, I would be able to agree with existing mandates and release them into the earth. I think this is similar to what some intercessors are already functioning in when praying in tongues and utterances in an engaged or trance like state. This is rather perplexing but has more to do with aligning my heart than my mind.

I was given about thirty scrolls the other day and wasn't sure if I could release the angels assigned to carry out mandates that I had no knowledge of. I was permitted.

I was given the scrolls by angels in a counsel room. In a previous encounter, I was going with our Father up through the canopy of angels and as an aside he said, "you have a counsel of seventy assigned to your life, seven from each of ten layers".

I have engaged with this counsel a few times, this time I went in to ask them about things they know they are waiting to do regarding functions they each perform. I apologized for not knowing their functions or not engaging with them. Then I asked if they knew some of their mandates, could we move forward with those, that they could be released to function? That was when I got the thirty scrolls from them. Every scroll pertained to my life and destiny.

I have also released scrolls that I didn't know what they were for specifically, for situations and circumstances for cities or nations as directed. I was aware that my agreement with the bench of three, in angels' court, became a fourth that opens a gate to be released through into this realm.

These are all mandate scrolls that I didn't write but were given to me.

I have traded scrolls I received in court like judgement papers and mandates in the treasury and some were planted in my garden. Some are just being stored in my mountain for now. Some I have put in my belly, and for some that required blueprints, I went to the court of war or strategy. Some were planted, some released and some traded, each scenario is different although functional patterns emerge. Every scroll you find, or are given, or you get from someone in heaven or an angel, will pertain to your destiny scroll in some way even if your part is simply releasing it. It seems to be the efficacy of heaven.

March 13

Jesus told me to trade all my divorce (or severing) judgement papers at the treasury. I did this and I was given a handful of jewels, which I gave to Jesus. He placed each jewel in a crown and gave me the crown. He said it was a crown of righteousness. This doesn't mean it is the same for everyone. I was prompted to ask him what to do with my copies of all these divorce judgement papers. I have had a few from the throne of grace when I was asking for help in my time of need, and the scrolls authorized my help so I took them to angels' court.

I have asked to see if certain things were on my scroll in the future, so I could know whether or not to pursue them and invest time and effort now.

We love because he first loved us.
1 John 4:19

Yet I hold this against you: You have forsaken the love you had at first. *Revelation 2:4*

Once we peel away the thoughts and intents of our hearts and have them judged, it seems that our purified desires come forth. Therefore, 'plans to prosper you and not to harm you' may not be plans you are aware of. Yet I believe they will line up with desires of your heart.

I believe that scripture in context is to lead us out of captivity. It is hard to see clearly when we are in captivity so I think it is more of an invitation for us to trust his goodness.

March 14

I have found a consistent deficit in my perception. My application of what I see or understand is generally too limited or small. As I chew and progress along seeking more insight, I have to re-adjust constantly. It makes me semi-reluctant to share knowing I will be shown more by the Lord, yet I am becoming quite good at unashamedly being wrong! I have traded desires of my heart (really painful to give up) in order to only carry what is on my scroll. Jesus gives me back what is required in the moment.

March 15

As a suggestion, do you know what it means to present yourself as a living sacrifice? If so, have you presented yourself to Jesus like this? As your high priest, He is worthy to open the scroll written on your heart. Often, for our own protection, we can only see the bit in front of us until we get ourselves judged and migrate our life (body, soul & spirit) under his blood and untether from 'other' governments and re-align with the government of our Father and the headship of Jesus. So, we remain open to his lead, because we can't see what we can't see.

March 16
You could ask him what you need to do. I often get to that question late, lol. There were a couple of things I asked about which I was told not to worry about, because it will all work out fine.

I still haven't heard, years later. I trust more now that I will be prompted to ask the right questions in the right timing.

March 18
I think that we are able to apply any scriptural law to our lives. I have seen a book of destiny, I only get shown one page at a time. The first page Jesus showed me was writing I couldn't read. When I asked what this was, he said, "this is the page you are on". My angels were there as well, and afterward, we went out of the big library to a portico and we sat around a table discussing and planning, although I didn't know what we were saying.

I asked a while later if I could see what comes next. We turned the page and it had a full-page picture. As I was about to ask about what it was, I went right inside the picture and came out on a horse in Scotland with a flag. I knew I was riding up a hill to place my flag on the top.

As I rode, I turned around to see a long line of children on horses riding single file behind me. At the end of the line was a perpendicular line of warrior-like angels as a rear guard.

When I reached the top of hill, I dismounted and planted the flag. All the children also encircled me and the angels formed a perimeter circle around us. Then I came back out of the picture and was back in the library.

Within a few months, I ended up taking a trip to Scotland (Wales, England and Ireland too). I hadn't planned to go, it was my husband who suggested it and I laboured over the idea of going. I traded the trip and my desire to go and then our Father told me "the trip is from me". Something I already knew, is that I am to author a series of children's books. God has been speaking to me for many years about this. I think I picked up a literature inheritance during my trip. The purpose and fruit of the books will be leading children to claim new territory.

Everything I am shown is about my spiritual growth, so a page is for a season and also directly applies to my life currently. I asked to see if a couple things were in my future so I could know if I was to put effort and time into them now. Jesus showed me the future timeline and I saw my business logo (bit different than what I had currently at designer). I ended up changing my logo, and proceeded with my business startup planning.

March 19

I hope it helps, the day to day stuff is more like how you would describe being led by spirit, more fluid and intuitive.

Honestly, I got so disillusioned after being a Christian for around twenty-five years and stewarding every revelation to the best of my ability, healing, deliverance, compassion and operating in the gifts. Then a young friend died of cancer leaving her husband and two boys under age five. My husband and I drove ten hours to go pray to raise her from the dead. We spent a couple of days in the morgue with her body. There were angels everywhere and storms raging outside. My friend remained dead. Something changed in me at that time, it was like everything I knew and that the church currently teaches, is simply not enough! I found myself desperate and so dissatisfied.

A new year rolls around and some of the prophets have the word of the year. The same words from twenty years ago, same every year, same every month - every word exalting me in my great breakthrough and new platform etc. I love the prophetic gifting and ministry, although I had to acknowledge it was falling short.

I was in this despairing place when my Father opened up a whole bunch of realms and gave me a glimpse. I was so overwhelmed and I began the new journey where I know nothing and want him to teach me everything.

March 22

I haven't done anything regarding banks although I presented a case for corrupt use of government funds in our country. I also asked for judgement on the sexually deviant agenda in our education system in government that is trying to defile our children. To clarify, the agenda not the people, and only after extensively having my house judged.

March 23

Ideally our desires and ideas should line up with his. I have found that the more I get myself judged, get untethered, come out from 'other' governments, that my desires have changed and purified in measure. I have a dozen ideas a day so this is really important to me. The best I can offer you at this point is, ask if the idea is on your scroll and ask if there is a blueprint you can see. Be patient, trade the idea and all that is connected to it. Be led forth in peace.

You can get judged for your bloodline and the new bloodline you and your spouse created with your children. You can ask that everything you see and understand in your ex-spouse's bloodline be judged, plead guilty on behalf of yourself and your ex-spouse for having sinned as one, and for the iniquity passed to your children. You can get everything judged that you can see and understand. Plead guilty and ask for judgement under the blood of Jesus, including your descendants.

Don't worry about the enemy, deal with your legal stuff first. Get judged, then divorced or severed from other governing spirits, then reposition under the government of your Father. Getting judged is the key. You are migrating your life and being and bloodline under the blood of Jesus. It is your covering and it speaks for you. Keep at it and things will begin to fall away.

April 1

My personal thoughts are that we all need help, yet there is a personal breakthrough in each individual's relationship with their Father, Jesus and Holy Spirit. By that I mean, many don't believe they can see and therefore they want to engage the help of others. Any testimony is helpful as we can all springboard off each other's revelation. Jesus has used what other people have encountered to show me many things that we are already in dialogue about.

The key in this, is to be taught by the lord. In our individual relationships with him, is where we are encountering and learning about heaven. I am a big proponent of self-responsibility. Part of the church age mindset, even kingdom age mindset, is that we subjugate our relationship with him to other people. That being said, even newbies can help one another along, it is discipling as peers, or 'one anothering'. It is valuable that we come into rank, serve shoulder to shoulder, understanding we are all powerful to think, believe and act as we choose, as sons of our Father's kingdom. This is my encouragement to us all.

We seem to progress in our questioning and wondering something like this:

> I have a scroll of destiny?
> What is a scroll?
> Where is it?
> How do I find it?
> Can someone help me find it?
> Is there teaching on this?
> Jesus, where is my scroll?
> Can I see it?
> I can't see...
> I can't see my scroll
> How do I see my Scroll?
> Jesus, can you show it to me?
> Saw something, was that my scroll?

We keep pursuing until we eventually see it, begin to revisit it, start to know it, forge a pathway and become acquainted with our purpose. All this is about our relationship with him and it progresses as our relationship deepens.

April 2

I think dialogue is healthy, we gain so much from each other. I am speaking primarily of mindsets that hold us back thinking we are dependent on others rather than the Lord. In the church, we have created dependency on others. I believe the key is to be dependent on our rabbi, teacher, high priest, Jesus and Holy Spirit and our Father. Then we function inter-dependently with one another.

The scripture comes to mind, *'you need not that anyone teach you but I myself will teach you by my Holy Spirit'.*

I don't believe you are 'touching God's anointed' to have an opinion. You are powerful to believe and scrutinize as you will, as is everyone. I know there are many false encounters, which is where we can help one another. Ultimately, we are led and guided into all truth by Jesus who is the Truth.

I believe we all need to bring our thoughts, opinions, mindsets and beliefs under scrutiny and judgement. It is how we migrate our lives under the blood of Jesus.

By false encounter, I mean people engaging realms that are not through Jesus, he is the gate and we go in and out and find pasture. You can be 'in the spirit' and not in the kingdom of our Father. Satan has a menorah of realms, the top three realms of his kingdom overlay the lower kingdom realms of our Father, (kingdom of earth, kingdom of God and the kingdom of heaven).

Satan isn't in 'heaven', the place of God's abode, where the throne room is. He isn't in Mount Zion where all the courts are, except mobile court which hangs in the kingdom realm between heaven and earth. This structural teaching is available on the Internet although you need to engage and ask Jesus to show you how realms are structured. If we do not know the difference, we can easily encounter things that may be fascinating but aren't of our Father's kingdom.

I also believe we should know how to verify encounters by the nine strings or the frequency of heavenly DNA. Father: justice, judgement and holiness, Jesus: way, truth and life, Holy Spirit: righteousness, joy and peace. If anything doesn't resonate then you are in the wrong realm. Does that help? The more we get ourselves judged, the less likely we are to be 'easily led' into a wrong realm.

For example, some people share encounters that they are exalted in and you can hear their need for exaltation and tell they were led into something by that. Pride resonates. We are exalted in heaven by our Father and others, yet it is so humbling and the honor is immense. Humility resonates. Does that help?

I have learned the things I just shared from a teaching that is widely shared and then I set my desire for understanding of these things. I have been feeling a strong fear of the Lord recently and it's really sobering!

April 3

I find we are less and less prone to deception and false encounter the more we get ourselves judged. We have to be willing to take every teaching, personal encounter and testimony to the Lord ourselves. It becomes way easier to know truth. I remember saying to a friend (after having been lied to a couple times in a short period), "do I have a sign on my forehead that says please lie to me?". Immediately I realized I did.

Then I had deception judged in me, for wanting a palatable version of truth, condoning deception, exalting myself above deceivers, being a deceiver, every angle I could think of and it produced much sight! Then I tethered to Truth, the spirit of Truth and the government of Truth.

April 3

I have been pondering why there is treasure in heaven and for what purpose. Currency and treasure here is a reflection of there, so I am curious and learning. I believe we can operate outside of Adam, toiling for provision. Where provision simply is, because it is provided. In the parable of talents - they were 'given' talents, no toil involved. The key was in how to multiply what was given. I think there are patterns in the old testament and the new testament and in heaven. As earth is reflection of heaven, I believe we can engage principles along the way, while holding the heavenly as our mark to press towards. Some principles are like interim steps, like a phased roll out or a compression chamber of sorts. Some principles with an immediate application, like Jacob's speckled flock, are innovative strategies to be implemented now.

As for the treasury in heaven, the reality of the earthly reflection of kingly wealth and national wealth, leads me to believe it is relevant in ways I haven't grasped yet. We need to understand the treasury house.

There are probably lots of steps. I want to know how to translate provision from heaven so I am seeking understanding around this.

April 4

I would advise that you not bench with anyone yet, as there seems to be some missing pieces in what you wrote. Firstly, everything needs to be done from a place of rest. To enter his rest, we cease from our striving. If you feel pressure 'to act', it is not from his rest. Perspective is so different when you are in his rest, so you need to enter there first. Also, everything we are to be functioning in is from nesting and reproducing in the tree of life. I think knowledge of evil is exactly that, knowledge of evil. We need to be aware what tree we are eating from. Only the tree of life brings life. Eating from the tree of knowledge of good and evil brings chaos and death, even if we feel exalted for a time.

And then there is truth. Our Father knows the end from beginning and nothing is a surprise. We can relax into his plan and fulfill our destinies while feasting at the table he has prepared for us in the midst of our enemies. He is not at the mercy of Satan's plan, nor are we. So, we can refuse to exalt Satan's plans by not continuing to frame them up, because we are powerful to choose.

The benefit of the members of the body needing each other is that we can discern corporately. Pursuing heavenly realms in the kingdom of our Father, is not passive nor as simplistic as 'for fun'. Without accessing, you can only deal with things in this realm which has proven mostly fruitless, not reproducing life.

Everything is accomplished in heaven first and then in this realm. Everything here is fruit from one tree or another. We must mature in this so we are functioning without a head of our own, because we are sacrificed, submitted and connected to Jesus' head. So, first things first.

1). Enter his rest
2). Nest in and eat from the tree of life
3). Drink the water and feast from his table he has prepared for us
4). Present yourself as a living sacrifice, which includes trading or sacrificing your vision or plan for his.

When we do these, love will overcome us and we begin to look more like our Father. It is this love that our authority flows from. Otherwise our 'desire' to govern, subdue and conquer, is corruption from chaos. I caution you in trusting your heart (thoughts) because of this scripture in Jeremiah 17:9 *The heart is deceitful above all things and beyond cure. Who can understand it?*

Our safeguard is the framework of his name. Trading everything for more of him and having the thoughts and intents of our heart judged under the blood of Jesus. I hope that helps.

April 19

Often, we can only 'see' or 'perceive' what our scroll might be from earthly perspective, which is an inaccurate viewpoint, so we can presume it will be daunting. When engaging with heaven and with our Father regarding our destiny, our purpose becomes the only thing we want to do both in heavenly realms and on earth. The things that hold us back in our thinking in this realm don't exist in heaven. That is hard to grasp from here.

April 19

Added note, when we declare a thing without submission to our scrolls, to our Father, and to his kingdom, it is soulish and wrong trading with some other god. We then agree (without knowing) to having our provision come from outside our Father's kingdom. When 'blessings' and 'finances' show up, we thank our Father for them all the while unaware of the trading with another god we did to gain that provision. Many are led to believe that the opposite of a poverty mentality is a prosperity mentality. I suggest they are both ditches on either side of the highway. There is sufficient abundant supply in our Father's kingdom and as sons, it is all ours, in him. I am speaking from experience on the thanking God for provision that didn't come from him.

There are painful hard lessons to learn when coming out from wrong trading and being governed by entities in the wrong kingdom. I have a bloodline full of success and wealth, as well as poverty, and there is wrong trading on both ends.

Okay, so I just went to pick up my tax returns from my accountant and had a revelation drop in the car on the way home, regarding favor. I was pondering how what seems like favor often has strings attached. I felt a ping of resentment towards those that I feel a debt from strings attached such as gratitude, relationship, or return favors. I thought of the scripture about *'having no debt to any man except the debt to love'*. I recognized I have been engaging with a 'false favor' where people bless you or give to you (not necessarily financial) but it comes with unspoken strings only to be realized after the fact.

Not only in their giving to us, but also in our giving. For example, having someone damage something of ours and not offer to fix it, pay for it, or replace it. Then later they offer a replacement (which wasn't the same so it didn't work out) and say they wanted to offer that to us as a 'blessing'. All that to say, I am having little pings of resentment that have been popping up in me from all these weird scenarios.

So, I went to court just now to get judged for giving with strings attached, for engaging in false favor, attributing this favor to God and for participating in any way with it. Then I petitioned to be severed from governing false favor and have all strings attached to my bloodline and our DNA be cut and nullified, cancelling debts of favor. Then I repositioned my husband and I and our bloodlines under the favor of our Father and his kingdom and as an outflow to also have favor with man. These scriptures came to mind, Luke 2:52 *And Jesus kept increasing in wisdom and stature, and in favor with God and men.*

Proverbs 3:4 *So you will find favor and good repute in the sight of God and man.*

Wow. I never saw that before, but now it seems so obvious when I look back over my life and see how all these apparent blessings or favor always turned sour down the road, or required some type of implied repayment of favor.

April 23

I would suggest that both spouses have freemasonry in their bloodlines as it is fortified through marriage and creating a new bloodline. There are some great resources on the Internet for freedom from Freemason DNA and related iniquity. If it's in your DNA record, you can even be in judgement of it and still tied, as the descendants have been trafficked and traded. Untether and keep getting what you can see of it judged. A simple way is to entangle with Jesus, Father and Holy Spirit and then it becomes more obvious. Yes, Freemasons are very obviously serving Satan as it is in their written material, but not as obvious to those at the lower levels. They mock the blind who join because they don't know what is going on.

I recommend that if you haven't seen results in your own freedom regarding masonry, do not cave in to pressure go up against it on behalf of anyone. There is no rush, God is in control and many are dealing with things at a higher level of trading. Seek understanding and wisdom first. There is no point in doing anything that isn't on your scroll, or isn't in timing with your scroll. I can confidently assure you that our Father would not mandate you to corporately

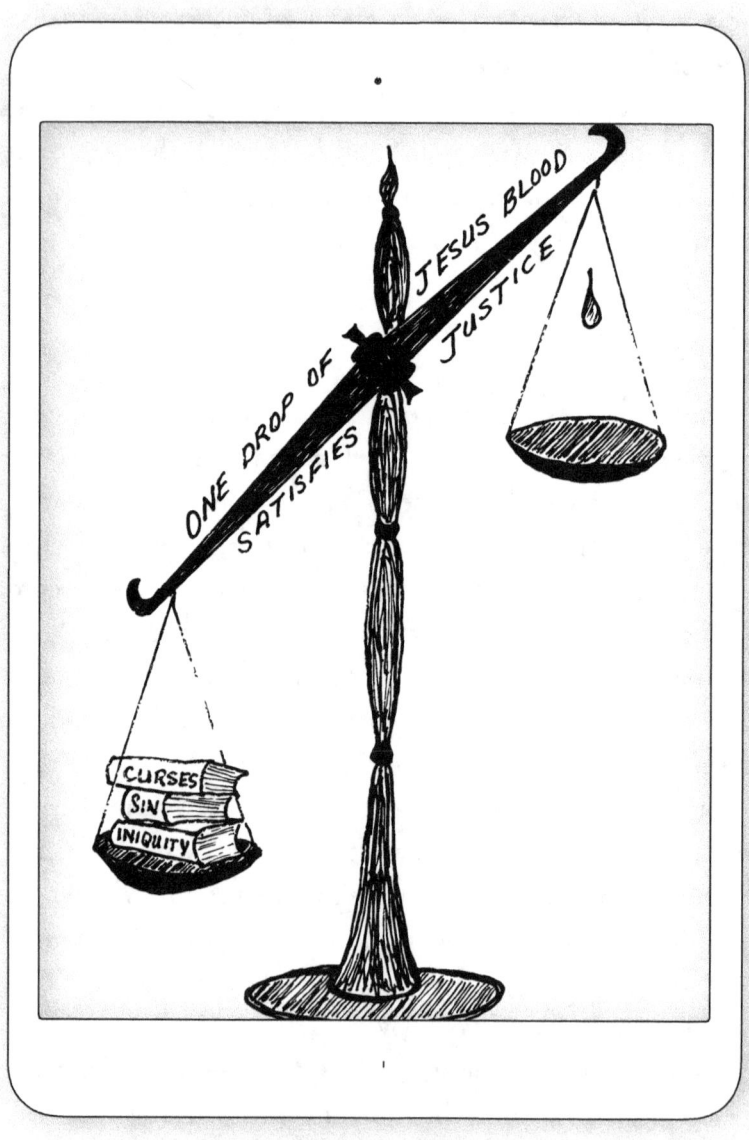

But about the Son he says, "Your throne, O God, will last for ever and ever; a scepter of justice will be the scepter of your kingdom". *Hebrews 1:8*

deal with this if you are not doing everything from His rest, and/or have not clearly untethered and legally come out from under its government as it can be dangerous. This scripture comes to mind, Proverbs 22:3 *The prudent see danger and take refuge, but the simple keep going and pay the penalty.*

Staying in line with your scroll, in our Father and in His love and in his name, is our refuge.

April 24

I always advise people to deal with what governs them first because our perspective changes so dramatically. It's hard to describe how dramatically our thinking changes and that everything we have ever known or believed, is a framework that our lives are filtered through. I have done deliverance for seventeen years and now, I don't even care about demons, they are the least of my concerns. My understanding of authority and hierarchy is so different now.

Most of what I 'heard' in what you shared, is that demons and ungodly governing spirits are a major focus for you. They are in your face, getting you and you are looking for the power to overcome them.

We overcome by the blood of the lamb and the word of our testimony. I think it's healthy to get off the battlefield, spend that effort on your own behalf by getting all those trading floors and iniquity judged in yourself first by the blood of the lamb.

Let your desire for justice and righteousness be governed by the seven spirits of God, by Jesus and let them teach you in all things. Seek wisdom and learn about the kingdom of our Father by spending time there with him. Let your desire to look like your Father be the word of your testimony as you come under the government of heaven and lordship of Jesus.

These are ungodly governments of ungodly or evil entities, trading on your bloodline and your DNA. The evil you see in this realm is fruit from another realm. That is why you deal with your record of iniquity in your DNA first. This is made clear in masonic texts and people's experiences in history. There are several ministries that have quality information regarding this. This is why we need the balance of intimacy and responsibility in our maturing process. We need the closeness and face to face relationship with Father, Son and Holy Spirit.

The picture is so much larger than recognizing illuminati control of economic and political power in this realm. We must mature in our understanding, authority and ability to govern. We mature by submitting every area of our being to the lordship and kingship of Jesus and by being humble and teachable. We bring our lives right under his blood as our refuge and covering. You are not an orphan as that too is a framework. Hope this helps.

April 26

I was just looking at two of my mountains yesterday. One of them, although a business mountain, I believe is connected to unlimited supply. The other is an ecclesia of sorts but more in regard to fathering or facilitating maturity in the body in order to become ecclesia or government. I was engaging the angels assigned to these mountains. I have been really desiring to move forward yet not seeing the next steps and so I was needing clarity on the blueprint. I needed clarity on my part of my scroll. One of my weaknesses is seeing things and not really knowing the timing, everything seems like it is now. I vacillate between engaging heaven, action in this realm, and waiting. I have given up many gifts and desires and possibilities because all these things had an element of 'identity' in them for me.

So, today I share the nugget of trading who you think you are, for who you are designed to be. For purity regarding your scroll of destiny. The ability to start from a blank page and let what is supposed to remain be given back to you as a purified desire.

I have always had a heart for the poor and I now know this is not on my scroll in any way I would have thought previously. If I hadn't traded my heart for the poor as part of my identity, I could have grabbed onto some really great ideas and opportunities and wasted time and effort outside of my scroll. I have a heart for the aging poor among us. Now I'm looking at completely different solutions, from a resource perspective, rather than a 'ministry' perspective.

April 27

I'll explain what I mean by resource versus ministry. There is an Asian couple in my community and they are in their sixties. They pick bottles from the garbage to make their living. Everyone in the community knows them and gives money to them. I befriended them several years ago. They came to Canada with the dream of a better life but they couldn't get decent jobs. They had a few entry levels jobs at the beginning and raised three children. They have been bottle picking for years and the wife has varying degrees of frostbite on her fingers, toes and cheeks because they are out every day through the winter picking bottles.

They haven't paid into a pension through employment and so they have nothing to even support them in old age. They rent a basement suite. I wanted to start a crowdfunding housing and retirement fund for them and market it in our community. I live in an affluent city and we should have our poor cared for easily.

Canada is cold in the winter with the exception of the west coast, which has similar climate to the west coast US, but it rains a lot. My husband and I once brought a man home on our anniversary that we met outside the restaurant we had dinner at. His feet were so messed up from being wet for days on end. We tried to get him a hotel room, but none of the hotels would take him as a guest because he had no identification, even if we paid!

Really what I want to do is form a national program for the homeless, I want to house them. I want them to have a refuge, a reprieve and to be cared for.

So rather than having a ministry to the poor, a feeding program or temporary shelter (which there are already many of), I want to fund private property, hotels or apartments, or retirement homes or something. Or come up with a workable solution through which, others can 'minister' to the poor.

I went to Haiti right after the earthquake and it was brutal. Beyond the devastation, I saw their poverty that was pre-existing. I saw garbage filled canals and the oceanfront was covered in plastic bottles and garbage. I prayed for healing for hundreds of people while I was there and I saw many miracles and healings.

Millions (billions?) was given in aid to Haiti that ended up in the hands of a corrupt government and port authority. They held shipping containers hostage at ports demanding hefty tariffs. I have a friend that lived there for a year or two after the earthquake and there were still warehouses of goods that never made it to the people in need and they all had hired security to protect them from theft. This is craziness.

I had an idea to start a recycling plant and create a program that would pay a price for every bottle and can on the ground, so the people could clean up their own island and be able to earn money. Then have a refundable deposit system on consumer drink packaging like we have here.

The recycling material could be compressed, shipped and sold off-island. I had also seen 'waste to energy plants' and thought that would make more sense for Haiti as their power grid there is in dramatically short supply. I am not sure if the garbage after initial cleanup would be enough to continue to power the island. But that wouldn't matter if the energy plants didn't need to profit. Waste to energy plants at the time cost approximately $100M. It would change the economy, provide jobs, provide an opportunity for day to day income for the poor, and provide power to the country.

If we can access an unlimited supply then business is simply a resource. Like electricity is a resource, water is a resource and food is a resource. I have ministered and loved in the one to one scenario because my heart is there. God so loved that he gave. His only son. It is his good pleasure to give, therefore it is my good pleasure to give. He gives us the kingdom and he gives good gifts.

I don't know if I accurately explained the difference I now see between ministry and resource, but I don't think I need to do another missions trip, or help at a feeding program. Other people have that on their scroll, it was just one of the ways I could express my heart for the poor.

By trading whatever part of my identity was tied to ministering to the poor, I no longer am distracted by that. It is good and godly, so I was okay with it in the past. My heart feels more purified now about my part in helping the poor. I could have carried on doing many things for the poor, in whatever way seemed good to me, but they are not on my scroll.

I have heard this said in varying ways in teachings, podcasts and conferences and I couldn't wrap my head around why healing someone might not be on my scroll. It feels as though my rest in him brings understanding that untethers me from a 'works equals identity' based mindset.

May 3

I consider most of what I engage in, that I'm not certain of or that I'm new at, to be 'practice'. I just keep engaging things and they open up more and more.

Often, I hear someone share something and think, 'wow, I didn't know that' or 'I haven't been there yet' and I set my desire to go check it out. I find this is super accelerated.

May 4

I will agree that I get clarification for myself as I share encounters and revelation. I find things I may have understood, but didn't realize that I did, begin to come out when I write it down to communicate with others. I have had some interesting encounters regarding treasury and finance that I have been chewing on for a while now.

May 10

I think the underlying mindset and heartbeat is 'care' for one another and a natural expectation to be 'cared' for. Without obligation or benefit except love.

Like we read in Romans 13:7-8, *Give to everyone what you owe them: if you owe taxes, pay taxes; if revenue, then revenue; if respect, then respect; if honor, then honor. Let no debt remain outstanding, except the continuing debt to love one another, for whoever loves others has fulfilled the law.*

May 16

I have heard great testimony of how two drops of lavender under the tongue daily acts as an anti-anxiety for depression.

Seeing is a natural outflow of clearing your gates and cleansing your DNA through getting yourself and your bloodline judged under the blood of Jesus. If you don't know where to start, there is a trading floor document on Jane's website and other places on the Internet. You can begin by pleading guilty to sins you and your ancestors have committed. This changes our thinking and mindsets fairly immediately.

Feeling, sensing and hearing are all valid in relationship with Father, Son and Holy Spirit. All senses grow with use so we just keep going deeper.

I think that all of our journeys into a deeper relationship with our Father are uniquely directed by him like the scripture that says, *a man's heart determines his path but the Lord directs his steps.*

There were things I could not have seen on my scroll because my mind wasn't renewed to be able to perceive them. There were things on my scroll that enabled deeper cleansing.

The closer I get in relationship with Father, Son and Holy Spirit, the clearer the delicate dance of my growth and maturing gets. The desire of oneness in him is way greater the more I engage.

May 24

I have been looking at a particular office space for lease for about a year now yet I have not progressed further on a physical business location. I have been waiting on clarity and timing as the blueprint is revealed more. In this past year, I have engaged angels on the property which is an old closed Canadian Forces Base and global air force training base. I often go to the property to engage and pray. It is part of a decade long redevelopment plan to create an auxiliary urban center in my city. The land is crown land and some of the buildings are designated with heritage status. I have also been looking at investing in a couple of condos nearby.

I have discovered a sacrificial altar buried in the ground from post ww2 that I had repented for and had judged. It was a gate and still releasing a frequency. I also had the governmental and military power seats judged as they have been held by masons as well as corrupt use of government military funds. This is recorded historical information I read about the land and what has transpired on it.

There is a crown corporation that handles the redevelopment and sale of crown land and I repented on behalf of our government and had our corruption judged there too. The leasing company that holds the contract for the crown held buildings on this development at the moment is named after a star. When I googled the star name I found a whole host of information about gods and functions. There are new age teachings that speak of a race of beings from this star so I went to have any ungodly trading with and on this star judged in me and in our Canadian government.

Today as I write this I am on the property, with a forecast of 100km winds. I felt to deal with this storm and googled the star name again and found it is connected to a Mesopotamian god of the storm. Our city is always and historically has been ravaged by storms, flooding, large hail, high winds and funnel clouds. I then saw our provincial devastation by weather and our national devastation by weather, so I had this judged as well. I will track the wind today to see results.

Anyway, I share all of that as I have wondered at the timeline on starting up my business. In finding this leased office space, I have uncovered and been dealing with many governmental issues. I have sensed this is significant although I am not sure what it is all unto. I had no idea what I was getting myself into when I first looked at this office space and I have been led to do all this stuff in seeing our sin as a city, a province, a military force and a nation.

A week or two ago, I saw a sign up for the sale of some of the crown land for residential use. After realizing the land is still for sale (utilities are laid and roads are developed), I then thought perhaps I might be able to purchase the building I like (and maintain requirements for heritage status) rather than leasing it.

Now it is a potential investment even though I don't have the ability to purchase this property on my own. I believe if it is part of the blueprint then it must be doable somehow even if I don't know how or can't see it at the moment. I haven't pursued the real estate broker to see if this particular building and property is for sale yet, but it wasn't until I took responsibility for the land, that this idea of purchasing even entered my mind.

May 25

I had an encounter a while ago where my mountain lifted up and all these laser lights shot out in multiple directions at the base of it. I felt this was building pillars under it and requires more understanding. I had already built an altar under it.

I still don't understand the function of pillars, if any have experience to share I would love to hear.

Yes, I think in the business legislation encounter we were under a mountain with pillars when we reviewed blueprints from Wisdom. Interesting. I knew I had to build an altar under my mountain and it came forth out

Whoever believes in me, as Scripture has said, rivers of living water will flow from within them.
John 7:38

…you can say to this mountain, 'Move from here to there,' and it will move.
Matthew 17:20

of my spirit, and I presented myself as living sacrifice on it. It involved much weeping. This was different from the other altar I have sacrificed myself on, or preparation by Jesus of me, the sacrifice. I'm not sure where those were.

June 3

I think this comment was about a dream someone in the chat group had. The government of leviathan is many headed, being the king of sons of pride. I would suggest that your 'house' has a 'door' open to it, and it is 'living' there. Because it is a governing spirit, it will be governing legally through the record of iniquity carried in your DNA from the sins of your ancestors. You can ask Holy Spirit to reveal what the sins are, where you and bloodline have traded with leviathan for provision, or for needs in your 'household' (meaning family line) and go to mobile court to get judged for the sin. Plead guilty under blood of Jesus, ask for the sins to be judged and the record in your DNA to be judged. Include your ancestors and descendants. Then petition to have the government severed or divorced from your household, and declare your submission to government of your Father.

Take the judgement of divorce scroll to angels' court and submit it for administration. Angels will go take care of the actual government 'structure' that was set up over your household, and deconstruct it as well as the severing ties. Then, you may see more of how this is operating and you can rinse & repeat.

I decided to write out the process as we all have this government in operation through iniquity and I'm not sure who has dealt with it or not yet. I hope that helps. This process of coming out from under 'other governments' and repositioning under the government of our Father is how we are ruling from our personal mountain. We are learning how to be a lord over our first sphere of governance which is our own life and family. A close friend in the dream that was shared was bringing something else in so it might also speak to unholy alliances. The presence of leviathan at the same time may be identifying the behemoth government as the two create an arc to govern through. Spirit pairing plus you, in agreement (through choice, agreement or iniquity record in DNA), create a bench of three. Just get all the sin, trading and record judged under the blood of Jesus.

June 5
I never registered my business in heaven although I did get a blueprint and then wrote out the business plan and budget and took it in for approval.

June 19
Identifying where you are at in the journey of discovering your scroll of destiny and your personal mountains will help you with next step so you don't camp on a bit of revelation.

For scrolls example:
> I've never seen my scroll or book, what do I do?
> I've encountered my scroll or book but couldn't read it or see what was on it.
> I've engaged with my scroll or book of destiny and have a general sense of purpose but nothing in detail.
> I have engaged with it and am wondering how to discern daily mandates.
> I discern mandates but am not sure what to do about them.

For mountains example:
> I have not seen my mountain.
> I have been shown my mountain but haven't known how to engage and rule from there.
> I have been dealing with the entities that are governing on my mountain but am not sure how to proceed.
> I have never seen my gates and thrones.
> I am dealing with my gates, Jesus is on my throne with me, I need to understand ruling on my mountain.
> I have seen several other mountains, am not sure what to do with them.

Present yourself to Jesus as a living sacrifice and ask him to open your scroll. Some people see a literal scroll, some a book and some see something like a hologram. I can generally only see a small season at one go or on one page. I personally have a book in a large library and we go through it one page at a time. It is pictorial and sometimes it has writing that isn't English that I can't read yet and every new bit is revealed by Jesus.

I have asked to see a couple certain things in future and was shown along a timeline to see their existence in future. They were both major aspects of my scroll, one was a business and one was authoring. I wanted to clarify I was on track rather than do something outside of my scroll.

June 20

So, to clarify what you are saying, you are coming up a mountain and you see a dragon, you take him out, then you see an open door and then an angel takes you to another mountain, and you saw the city from the second mountain.

I think first mountain is yours, there was a dragon governing until you took him out and this opened access to heaven through the door in your mountain. The next mountain might be Mt. Zion and I am not sure on which city as there are many. If you go up the first mountain, there should be a throne on top. You ask Jesus to take the throne as your lord and king and then you take a seat inside him. He will teach you how to be a lord for your mountain of your life in submission to his lordship.

I have noticed a nice blend of setting my desire to see things and any of the Trinity showing me things they want to reveal to me. I seem to get shown what I call precedent encounters, where I experience things beyond my understanding. Then I pursue understanding by re-engaging over and over.

I generally engage heavenly realms when listening to podcasts so what I am hearing, I am experiencing as well. This often leads to some type of personal encounter where I am governing something, dealing with stuff or pursuing understanding. I collect bits I hear on teachings for further exploration. I feel these all flow into my desire and become a pool of wonderings that I draw from when in heavenly realms.

I find I engage when I dialogue as well. It seems to be more of the seven spirits of God when talking with others and is really revelatory, like a swirl opens up into other realms and I see, sense, experience as I'm talking and listening. Singing worship songs corporately is the easiest access for me and I engage without trying, it just happens. When checking in with my scroll it is always Jesus and I and four angels assigned to me. Is that what you were asking? I go at will to accusation court and angels court whenever I feel led or know that I need to. I go to other courts at will too, but generally I feel or sense a mandate to accomplish something first. Sometimes I am escorted there as an introduction so I can continue to engage there.

I have heard varying experiences of what people have encountered on their mountains. Some see dragons, giants, ogres, goats and creatures. The main thing is to understand that these have been ruling you on your mountain, robbing you and hindering you. Once you get on your throne with Jesus, he teaches you how to govern from there for every area of your life.

I have also heard varying experiences with regard to personal mountains. Some see these mountains right away and others are revealed in time and readiness. Some see separate mountains for different areas of their life for example; finance, relationships, family, business or occupation, health, ministry and more. Some people see their mountains merge or stack into one larger mountain and some see their mountains expand and grow.

June 21

Side note*** dragons and others have eaten treasure that was meant for you. You can recover this. Slit open their bellies with your sword or with light from your belly and get the treasure and go trade it with Jesus or Melchizedek if you have met him. You can also mandate angels to retrieve it for you or petition in court for restitution, there are multiple ways so proceed as you are led. This is an overcoming step to understanding a ruling position. I always just ask what to do next because really, who knew any of this? Jesus or Wisdom are usually with me and walk me through what to do.

June 26

Submission to your destiny is being a living sacrifice. The more we engage with our destiny, the more settled and fulfilled we are. Honestly what I can tell you is to keep re-engaging your scroll. Go with Jesus everywhere you mentioned including mountains and ask him about all of it. Some examples of questions could include; Jesus, why is this wine by my book? What do I do with it? Drink it? Share it? What do I do with this dragon? What is it governing? Daily is good but if you are not in a daily routine of engaging heaven, then steady as she goes. It is a relationship. One thing I would recommend is tending to your mountain with Jesus as it will accelerate all your other understanding about burdens. Knowing your scroll will eliminate any distraction burdens you are not meant to deal with.

June 27

Yes, sometimes I 'see' things overlaying the natural realm (more than one realm at a time), generally it is something that is being revealed to me. I have seen people's faces morph or transpose and then I keep pursuing what it's about.

July 3

I have a light structure that surrounds me like a dome on top of my mountain. It's a geometric shape though. This fingerprint is very interesting, did you get any sense of what it is for? Like what it's function is? That's an interesting concept because our fingerprints are unique, it never occurred to me that they would be a reflection of one big network, nice insight. I'll have to explore that further.

We can govern our surroundings by ruling from our mountain, you overtake your immediate vicinity as a government. My personal mountain is larger than my property, so in the spirit it encroaches a bit to my neighbors.

What is man that you are mindful of him?
...You have made them a little lower than the angels and crowed them with glory and honor.   *Psalm 8:4-5*

July 17

Because our individual relationships differ, the answer to your question isn't simple yet, he wants us all to know our destiny and walk in it. If you ask, or set your desire to know your scroll there are generally some things required such as submitting your life as a sacrifice and positioning under the headship of the one who is worthy to open the scroll, Jesus.

I have found this to be progressive in deepening our relationship with Jesus, Father and Holy Spirit. Some things you will 'know' you are called to, as you have already experienced the delight of pursuing a path in life, or deeper fulfillment in a certain activity or career or interest.

Basically, we begin to trade our lives for our destinies, as we grow in desire to only do 'what we see the Father do'. It is him who works in us to will to do his will. I have wondered about the terminology of 'landing a scroll' as I think many simply parrot terminology without understanding. Other ministries use this terminology and my observation is that they are petitioning for the destinies of nations to be released. They are petitioning in the higher courts for a specific purpose. My current understanding of the term 'landing' means receiving a scroll and releasing it into this realm.

At a simpler level, I was attending a church a few years ago and was on the leadership team. We were beginning a leader's meeting with worship at the pastor's house. I went to see Jesus and he gave me a scroll for the church. I asked what to do with it and we ended up in Angel's court. I submitted the scroll for administration and four angels showed up for mandates. They were then each given a scroll and released through me. Three went off in different directions and one came into the room I was in.

When I asked his name and what he was doing, he said his name which wasn't English but sounded similar to an English word. He said he would stay with the pastor from then onward and he would go wherever the pastor goes. Then he sat at their kitchen table and told me he would eat with them and live with them.

After this encounter, I asked Jesus why I was given that scroll to release and not someone else as I was kind of cranky about some things at the time. He said it was because I carry them in my heart. I was a bit wrecked.

Yes, you begin changing the government of your life, some by submission, some by usurping. If you have not been ruling in your gates, something from your bloodline will be. First you oust that, and submit that area to Jesus and then he teaches us how to rule our lives. For every trading floor and trading entity that you divorce or sever from, you then submit that area to the government of our Father. This is changing the governance of your mountain. You start with your own personal mountain for your being and your life.

For me, I was at my choice gate with Jesus and Wisdom and then the whole diagram of gateways shot up like a cone or mountain and we all were on top by a throne.

There was a huge dragon there and although it was not on the throne, it was in front of it with its tail curled under its body and was touching the throne. I beheaded the dragon and slit its belly open and took out these orb things and went and traded them with a man at the sea of glass. He gave me a torch and told me to go and put it into the belly cavity. I went back and put the torch in the belly cavity and the dragon exploded. Then I realized there was a whole crowd of angels and people cheering loudly. They were so happy for me. I was too. Since then I have occupied my throne with Jesus. I am learning to rule every aspect of my life from there including my gates.

I have a business mountain that showed up after I got a business blueprint and I govern my business from there. I have a ministry of sorts and had been many places in encounters that I didn't know where I was specifically and then one day I was shown they were inside a ministry mountain. Others seem to see their mountains sooner, clearer, and orderly, so I can only relate my personal experience. Can others share testimony?

July 19

I have been considering the banking idea that came up last year because I ran across an article of the top five offshore banking jurisdictions. The idea is to have a private offshore bank (typically used for tax evasion or laundering corrupt funds), in order to have a 'private' bank that functions within the current banking laws. Someone must be going to do something similar to this in the future because it's a good idea.

How to get a blueprint and a strategy to implement the blueprint? If you ask Father, Son, Holy Spirit et al. how to get a blueprint, then you can begin to frame from there. We may also be able to simply be available for business and therefore be given ideas because we are willing to take responsibility for them. I haven't sorted that all out yet so I am not sure how it can work.

July 20

You can check out the body, soul and spirit gateways information that is available to get a framework. The gate of first love is good to see first. Ask Jesus to begin to show you what needs to be done as we may have well-worn pathways established in our being where we connect with heaven already. Worship seems to be a common clear gate and for others it is thankfulness or faith. Something you find easy already as you have established a path to connect with the Trinity throughout your relationship.

We go through many different coronations and investitures as we progress in maturity, authority and responsibility. This is personal for each one of us yet there are some commonalities. See Jane's website at www.oneunitedbody.org there is a page with information on lords to kings to sons.

My personal experience is the more time I was in mobile court getting myself judged for agreeing with ungodly governance in my life, the clearer I could see and the more I could understand. For example, I would get judged under the blood of Jesus for agreeing with use of trading with and into, control and manipulation. Then I would get divorced or severed from that and reposition my bloodline, life and being under the government of my Father. We confess sin and get judged under blood. This is to repent and turn, which means severing ties and asking for that government to be judged around our life as well. Then we connect to our Father's government of his kingdom. It brings immediate change in your thinking because you are renewing your mind and this shifts circumstances around you. This is part of the process of dying to self.

July 21

I think our redemptive gifts from Romans 12 tie into our identity issues, but like all things it can become replacement for our identity from our Father. I have seen people use redemptive gifts or motivational DNA to stay identified in their junk or immaturity, rather than being solid in who they were created to be by our Father and maturing in that. It really was quite affirming for me to identify how I am wired and I have had friends who just wept when they saw how they are wired as many wounds come from trying to meet others' expectations of us.

I have seen people settle into great confidence to be who they are and how they are motivated. Understanding redemptive gifts or motivational DNA illuminates lies about our identity very clearly. Like all things, it goes into my pool of understanding to be drawn from as I live out my scroll. I can problem solve like nobody's business (not always my own though), yet I need to know when to not get wrapped up in solving problems that aren't mine to solve. Sometimes because it's not on my scroll or because it's feeding some ungodly fulfillment of identity that is false. Does that make sense how our identity and destiny go hand in hand?

July 21

I was just listening to a teaching podcast and heard it mentioned how our Father is white light, and the light prisms out into seven colors as the seven spirits of God. Then it was shared how we are taught by the seven spirits how to be all white light again. This means each one teaches us their part so we can be all parts. It is an interesting correlation to the seven redemptive gifts and how the fullness of being one with Jesus should have us proficient in all because we would be all like he is.

July 22

The benefit of each person sharing their experiences, questions and understanding is that it aids in keeping out a religious framework. Over time, noticeable patterns of similarity emerge as well as the variety of personally being taught by the lord and hosts of heaven. It makes it obvious that there is not a religious idea that we all 'have' to experience same things to be 'legitimate'.

I find it fascinating how we are all taught so differently! We all get to springboard off each other's revelation, promoting some acceleration in a healthy functioning body.

July 27

I have been seeing some stuff lately connected with Solomon that is not only about accessing unlimited supply but understanding how to create the supply as well. I have some large financial requirements if I am to purchase a commercial building and only recently upped my game so to speak. I have not confirmed if this is on my scroll yet although I am open to the responsibility now which I wasn't before. Also, I would need more than only finances. I believe I engaged Melchizedek one time and he reached inside me and took out my heart. The question came to mind wondering why he was doing this as I was shocked at what was happening. Then the scripture about where your heart is, there will be your treasure also reverberated through my being and I was settled in peace.

July 28

I am sharing resources because any of these things you can personally engage. Someone led a group through the initial process and he explained how some things are standard although they are not always in the same order and there are differing levels of detail and experience. For example, some teach seven lord mountains. I have only experienced one mountain that I govern every area of my life. I have a ministry of sorts that is its own enterprise and it has its own mountain. I only saw my business mountain when I received a blueprint for my business as it didn't exist before, it was created. So, perhaps I have seven mountains and don't see them as individual because I was okay to govern and submit my life from one throne.

Others have experienced individual mountains expanding and growing bigger and seven lord mountains merging like stacking cups. King mountains are revealed as you are functioning as a king and some have experienced these stacking as well, all into Mt. Zion. All that to say, wherever and however you are led is personal and the Trinity engage with us in our personal understanding. Our combined experiences offer the breadth needed to make room for others because we springboard off of each other's revelation and experience.

July 31

My answer is yes, we definitely can do many things in different ways. You can also explode light out of you which is very powerful as well. I love that your mountains are in a circle and I haven't heard that shared before.

Aug 1

I have speculations on the geometry of mountains although I have never seen a complete picture so I can't confirm anything at the moment. I have seen some mountains in a range of seven. I have seen them grow bigger and I have seen mine grow from a circle into a cone. I have also seen them as four-sided pyramids and have seen mountains as cubes. I have seen mountains lift up and grow while creating multiple mountains underneath and I have seen them move. I have wondered about living stones and being a temple. It seems I collect bits of info because I expect it to fit into a structure when revealed at some point because it's how I process information.

I have also danced on top of a range of mountains with Jesus which was really fun. I live right beside the Rocky Mountains and regionally, Jesus and I have been on top of those jumping and twirling from peak to peak.

Awesome! I think way more children are seeing inter-dimensionally than their parents are aware of. I have found that most people seem to be okay with and use the terminology of dreams and visions. When I am sharing with anyone that is familiar with the prophetic stream, I will use the word encounter as that is accurate and palatable. If I say I went to heaven, some people don't have a grid for that and I find it is a distraction in a conversation. I'm not concerned with what they think necessarily, but honestly sometimes terminology helps us connect to others and keeps revelation open so I choose that instead.

People have encounters in worship, encounters in prayer, encounters in dreams, encounters at salvation and I have found that most adults (in charismatic circles at least), seem to be more connected than they are aware of.

Aug 2

As parents, all of our children are on our scrolls as there is day to day destiny. It is not like key points or goals so going to the grocery store is also on your scroll.

There is a podcaster who describes this beautifully on many podcasts on heaven. He describes flowing where the joy is, where the peace is or where the bliss is. Mostly we would describe this as 'being led by the spirit'. It is as important to get daily mandates as it is to get the larger 'seemingly more purposeful' picture. I experience daily mandates intuitively as my book is in seasons or times (a couple of months per page), and I only see the page I am on presently. So far, I haven't seen the 'big' picture of my life.

I have been really desiring to know more, yet I am also content with how Jesus reveals things to me. I seem to wake up 'in it' so it is becoming a natural outflow of functioning in heaven at the same time as here. I do generally always see, sometimes I sense or feel or have motivation for things. Sometimes a window opens in my day to consciously engage and do something governmentally and I feel this is what I am to do right now. Okay, so after sharing all this, it occurred to me I haven't seen a new page in my book for quite a while.

Last month I went to a conference. The setting for the conference was in the country and the view from the picture windows in the facility was the exact picture of a view in my garden in my heart. I was so stunned and did not know what to make of it. I had never been to this geographical location before. Just now I asked Jesus to see another page and we met in my garden. Then we went into the library where my book is but from a different entrance this time. It was the same scenario with lots of tables in the middle of a room with my book open on a table, and Jesus and I were looking at it with my angels surrounding us.

As we turned the next page, I saw a full-page picture of a tree. On the tree were scrolls like fruit that was really ripe and some were falling off onto the ground. My first thought was the function of fruit is to carry seed in order to reproduce. The fruit cares for the seed until ripe and then drops off and successfully transitions into the ground below. I saw that the scrolls on the tree were people and destinies. As I wondered who and what all these ripe fruits scrolls were, I felt Jesus say they are relationships.

I stepped into the tree and became one with it and literally felt my own heart for people which is also his heart for these people. It felt like a rush of love or an exhale to release the fruit scrolls. Many scrolls were already fully ripened and on the ground yet the branches were still laden with more. It seemed as though this is a season of fruitfulness coming full term and of release for the tree in satisfying a purpose. I pondered who all these people are and then came out of the encounter as my personal messenger alert went off.

I had received a message from a person I have known for ten years or so. She was letting me know that her seven-year-old daughter just started speaking for the first time a couple months ago as a miracle. She wanted to share her joy and thankfulness with me. I have only seen her a handful of times in all these years and our relationship has been based on prayer and navigating life circumstances. As I was pondering this breakthrough in her life I was shown she was a fruit scroll on the ground. I began to weep,

...and provide for those who grieve in Zion, to bestow on them a crown of beauty instead of ashes, the oil of joy instead of mourning, and a garment of praise instead of a spirit of despair. They will be called oaks of righteousness, a planting of the Lord for the display of his splendor. *Isaiah 61:3*

realizing these fruit scrolls are all people that I have carried in my heart. This is quite overwhelming as I did not realize I have been holding people in my heart in this volume.

Anyway, I am looking forward to seeing (with understanding) what I have been doing in daily mandates for years. For the past year, every night I have been going through the gate of rest into the night and then through the gate of mystery into darkness. I only realized last night I have skipped doing this before falling asleep for the last month or two so I re-engaged this again last night. I too have a mountain for mysteries hidden in darkness or it is hidden in mystery.

Aug 5

I suspect although have not confirmed yet, that our mountains are expanding geometric shapes. It doesn't have to follow 'space' laws in that, if you put seven into one it is seven times as big. Some seem to go right inside each other (like they are absorbed), and some seem to maintain their own space and shape. Some have experienced their mountains stacking like Russian nesting dolls. There are an awful lot of geometry related teachings out there in varying religions, philosophies and mythologies. I think, although some patterns may resonate as true, they are structures in a wrong realm and are corrupted geometry. This is a quick presentation of some basic concepts. I believe that threads of knowledge run through all major religions. Although things appear similar, I don't swallow the whole bite without personal revelation.

I tried using the terminology 'Metatron's Cube' to describe something I encountered and it didn't sit right with me. Upon evaluation, it turns out the geometric shape I encountered is not the same shape as the one known as Metatron's Cube. There is a lot of higher knowledge being released at the moment, out there in the world, and we need to stay solid on what our Father is revealing. We need to be certain we are not eating of the wrong tree in order to be like God.
WE ALREADY ARE LIKE HIM.

This seems like a great time to insert a quick bit on triggers. If you find you are prone to just accept other religions' teachings because they are similar, or get fearful if anything looks new age, or like an eastern religion, or want to accept mystic teachings because they are ancient or Jewish, go to mobile court and get yourself judged. Get judged for not knowing truth, for believing false teachings, for rejecting truth because of fear and accepting knowledge as a belief. For doing all this in substitution of relationship with him and with his truth and his revelation.

Be willing to have been wrong, willing to not know and not compromise regarding truth so that you don't make a lie your refuge. Then reposition your life and being under the headship of Jesus, the government of Jesus who is the way, the truth and the life. This is so liberating.

Aug 8
Yes, that is the right track. We begin to get mindsets judged in us and establish ourselves under the government of truth.

We have our wrong trading judged and end trading relationships. It seems to be a personal process with the Lord as things are revealed to us.

I know I have unbelievers on my scroll because I have a heart for people to know who Jesus is and it is his heart as well. I also know my role is at a different place right now in the timing of it so it is not a focus at the moment.

Aug 9

His kindness leads us to repentance. I think there is a healthy fear of the lord that can see that he will not be mocked or share his glory. There are things he has said in scripture we need to take as seriously as his kindness. There is scripture of sin that we are not even to pray for forgiveness on behalf of someone, in certain circumstances. This causes a deep reverence in me to know and understand my father. I can't remember the reference off the top of my head, does anyone know the scripture I am referring to?

I am wondering if any in the group here have maybe seen their mountain, but not engaged the throne on it? And what if any, obstacles are you encountering in ruling as lord from your mountain? I was getting the sense that we are in a grace for ruling right now, meaning if you present your obstacles that there is overcoming help available. I'm feeling it like a flow right now, and sensing the seven spirits are eager to help us move forward.

Have you been over or above your mountains like as if you are brooding? Sometimes things required come from that experience. Sometimes I go over my mountains like from above and expand over them and love them. Have you occupied your personal throne? Have you encountered it as a mobile throne yet? Like the throne in Ezekiel's description? Have you been on top of your mountain as a lord with Jesus? If not, you can meet him there and ask him to sit on your throne, then sit inside him. You will go right inside him, him right inside you. Like two people inside one body.

So yes, this throne is mobile, as you engage elsewhere or different mountains your throne goes with you. You can go sit (with throne) on king mountains and ask what is next? You will get a sense of different things relating to the mountain and some require action and some don't. Even if you are shown something seemingly unrelated, pursue it anyways. I have done some surprising stuff from just pursuing what comes up in hanging around on a mountain. You access them by setting your desire to go to your mountains and yes, do. You can also go to angel's court and ask for any scrolls for the mountain, or for his timing. You will usually find some men in white linen or others in heaven have stuff prepared for you. Even regarding personal mountains, I usually feel a nudge to go get a scroll that is already approved and waiting in angel's court. I connect with Jesus first, in my garden or the throne room or somewhere and then we go from there.

Aug 11

I wrote this as a post full of emojis to help summarize and lighten some heavy topics. I am posting this again as it is a good summary of how we position and tether to the government of heaven under headship of Jesus.

We come into authority in Christ right away, and then grow into positions of authority and responsibility. One of those positions is self-governance, ruling our personal mountain with Jesus ruling our spirit, spirit ruling our soul, soul ruling our body, from the inside out. Submitting ourselves to Christ and letting him teach us how to rule ourselves.

All the cleansing from our bloodline iniquity includes:
- trading floors
- altars of sacrifice in the earth and this realm (Nephilim, blood, seed and finance)
- covenants within contracts
- seed line DNA trading
- star trading
- untethering from the terrestrial and celestial influences
- restoring crowns in scripture
- killing kings of the kingdoms of the world
- booting out familiar spirits
- restoring gateway rulership
- presenting ourselves as living sacrifice
- killing serpents, dragons and giants

...and it is all about our mountain first, (personal, family, health, finance etc.) and then other mountains as they pertain to our scroll.

Our rulership in every area needs to come out from under whatever it is connected to, submitted to, covenanted with, tethered to, ruled by, and recorded in our DNA. Because this is a process that happens on a spiral of revelation, we clean as we go. I believe this is what sanctification truly is, becoming like him.

And it is nonlinear, not like first this then this, but led very personally in intimate relationship with our Father, Jesus, Holy Spirit, all of our teachers in heaven, angels to help, and those in heaven who have traded into our destinies for fulfillment. This is all dealt with in the judicial and legislative system in heaven as we are cleansed by his judgement under the blood covering of Jesus.

Aug 11

We go to mobile court and plead guilty to all the sinning with ungodly things governing us. We ask to be judged under the blood, and for our bloodline to be judged as well. Then we petition for severing governmental ties and we reposition our life and being under the government of our Father under the headship of Jesus. Let Holy Spirit or Jesus show you where to start. You can do this on your own with him and it is an ongoing process.

You can meet Jesus in your heart and go from there, or set your desire to access mobile court and look or sense for Jesus when you show up. As soon as you hear anything shared that piques your interest, ask Jesus to show you more about that throughout your day.

There can be super fast-tracking in confidence that he wants to show us everything because it brings him delight.

It can be overwhelming to think you need to cover every year and every generation and we expand our understanding as we go. So, if you understand you are functioning as a priest on behalf of your bloodline, for yourself and your descendants (the bloodline you created), then it can be done in large groups as you understand the trading involved.

Example: you can have every possible trade on trading floors (like with Jezebel), judged. This is all ungodly trading into manipulation and control to get our needs met rather than having our Father meet all our needs according to his riches in glory. This also includes a lust for power and ungodly means to obtain it.

Jesus and Holy Spirit can show you what is left undone. As our understanding increases we continue to get judged to the level of our understanding. I am saying that because it can seem like a daunting task but it really isn't. In words to explain it seems like a bigger task than in actions when you do it.

Aug 11

I have been looking at finance and watched some YouTube videos from some ministries that are getting revelation around financial grids. I keep seeing a separate financial or provision system like a layer over the earth. It hasn't been revealed to me yet though.

Basically, when we have been talking about taking yourself off the grid, this can be done by pleading guilty to wrong trading and wrong everything regarding provision. Get yourself judged. Removes trades. Have trading with the king of Tyre judged as all the mason bloodlines trade their descendants. So just plead guilty and ask for removal, so nothing is robbing your personal treasury. The converse is true as well, we don't want our treasuries filled by wrong trading either. Wrong or ungodly trading hides easier in abundance as we think we are blessed by God.

Aug 12

I was discussing once about how simply being available and obedient has us doing governmental things we didn't know were mountains, or even on our scroll. They seem to be 'one off' type mandates. I then joked about how there are so few accessing heaven that heaven will take anyone who shows up to fulfill something. Like on a podcast I heard, it was described that someone in a hub group was in heaven and was asked to sign off on something and then told after that it was for an earthquake.

Aug 13

Yes, if we are being inundated with demonic activity it means we have our own stuff to deal with. It serves as an indicator that it is time to close some gates off and take back rulership of areas of your personal mountain. Everything should be done from a position of resting in him. Otherwise we are kept busy fighting from the wrong realm and it keeps us in a victim position. Then it becomes all you see and focus on and it gets more exaltation than our Father. Something to note in our day to day life is that when we are not on our mountain, resting in his authority, our number one priority is getting there in him, not warfare. It seems counter-productive yet it is the way out of warfare battles.

Aug 15

I rule my personal life from one mountain, although I have a business mountain and ministry mountain, I feel these are more king mountains as they come with a domain beyond my personal scope. Sometimes mountains merge and grow although I have never heard of one shrinking before! Yet maybe what you suspect you are discerning is the case, it is you who are getting bigger rather than the mountain getting smaller.

Aug 16

The interesting growth dynamic is that the more responsibility you are willing to take on in heaven, the faster you grow. The more you grow and mature, the more responsibility you want to take on.

Aug 20

I listened to a livestream last night of a really humble man and part of his sharing included his walk with the Lord in trading the desires of his heart. He considered this to be trading into his own destiny. So powerful! I have found this to be a pattern where we finally see our scroll or part of it and it reaffirms the desires in our hearts. We allow them to come to the forefront and then we have the opportunity to trade them for his desires. We choose.

Aug 22

In the group business encounter I received a personal administration angel which I think is partnering with three I already have assigned that are builders and architects. I had a bench of seven from the court of the upright for my blueprint appear in a counsel room and I engaged them personally after group encounter.

Sept 9

I have a couple of local friends that I am on a bench with. We engaged one night together and were taken through an officiating type ceremony as we were formed as a bench. It started in the court of the fathers, then went to king's court and chancellor's court and then court of scribes, then to angel's court. We were taken through by Wisdom. I don't know that every process is the same although that was our experience. Generally, I engage when I feel led by a mandate from within my spirit, then I go see what to do about it. Various cloud of witnesses will agree on a mandate, almost like a bench for the moment because of agreement and it seems informal in the sense that it may be only for one thing. Or at least one thing I am privy to.

Sept 24

I wanted to share how some daily mandates play out in my day to day. Some people may use different language other than mandates as it seems fairly official sounding for acts like calling a friend, staying home, going to the grocery store or work. Some people use other terms like divine appointments or an unction or being led by the Spirit. Mandate simply means authorized to do a thing or even be a thing. I have an ongoing mandate for conflict resolution. I don't always know clearly what conflicts are going to come up or my part in them if any, but I see my Father's hand each time this happens. This may seem odd as I am not super great at resolving my own conflicts.

It may be as simple as deciding to go to a specific grocery store and bumping into a friend's senior father. He and his English as a second language friend had been waiting for a cab for longer than normal. I called the cab company and they said their computer showed the two seniors were picked up and the trip was complete. I offered them a ride and we were about to go out the doors when a cab came for them. They took it. Now the only conflict I helped with was speaking clear English to the dispatcher so he could then evaluate what went wrong within their system and resolve that himself. I also offered the people a ride which they did not need. Problem solving when people need it is part of my scroll. In the moment, I have to check in to see if I am supposed to help or not. These are daily mandates.

Some days I run across a bigger issue that requires governance of some kind. One area is child welfare. In this case I would do whatever governmental thing is required that day. For example, legislating righteousness into specific local government office or calling for corruption exposure so that legally in this realm something can be done to benefit the welfare of children. Then I follow up by checking what happens in this realm and what shows up in news after.

Sometimes I am led into dealing with things that weren't on my heart, yet my start point was something of concern or desire. It's a path of things revealed. Another example would be that I see a weird street name and go home and google it. Then I find out there was a historical issue that leads back to a group of people somewhere else that leads to a current day business or environmental issue. I then do what I see that I am to do about it. I may have only had the historical issue in my heart yet it is only part of the picture. I was led into something in my Father's heart. Part of relaxing into our daily scroll is functioning from the seat of rest. We enter his rest and cease from our own striving. It is a complete shift in what frames my identity, worth, value and importance. His delight is my delight and my delight is his delight.

Nov 7

Hey all... I'm moving into new season of my scroll and that includes ending my participation in most chats. I will stay connected in a couple and haven't totally decided which ones yet but I will be leaving this scrolls and mountains chat. I felt this when I went away for a week last month and my life began transitioning in a few areas. Thank you so much for including me, it has been a treasure to discuss and share with all of you.

I feel as though I am to move forward on some aspects of business now. I have registered my domain name. I need to incorporate shortly and start nailing down some intellectual property agreements, non-disclosures and collaborative contracts. It is such a season shift! I just ended monthly coffee meetups I have been organizing in my city for last year as well and I am not sure what is next with that either.

Jan 16 - The Final Post

In response to a page written on Jane's website about deploying too early, I think this also applies in the sense of 'arriving' at a point in individual destiny. Something is revealed on our scrolls and we camp out there as if we have arrived at our purpose. I have watched a pattern emerge in the heavenly realms community on the Internet. Some begin engaging heaven and find a renewed sense of calling. Then without a new grid or even by some revelation with a newly changed grid, they launch a ministry of teaching others about heaven. In this case the activity is deploying for battle without seeing the battle. We continue to be humbled as we love our lives not unto death, sometimes publicly and sometimes privately.

It reminds me of Rick Joyner's Final Quest vision where the objective was to engage the mountain of the Lord,

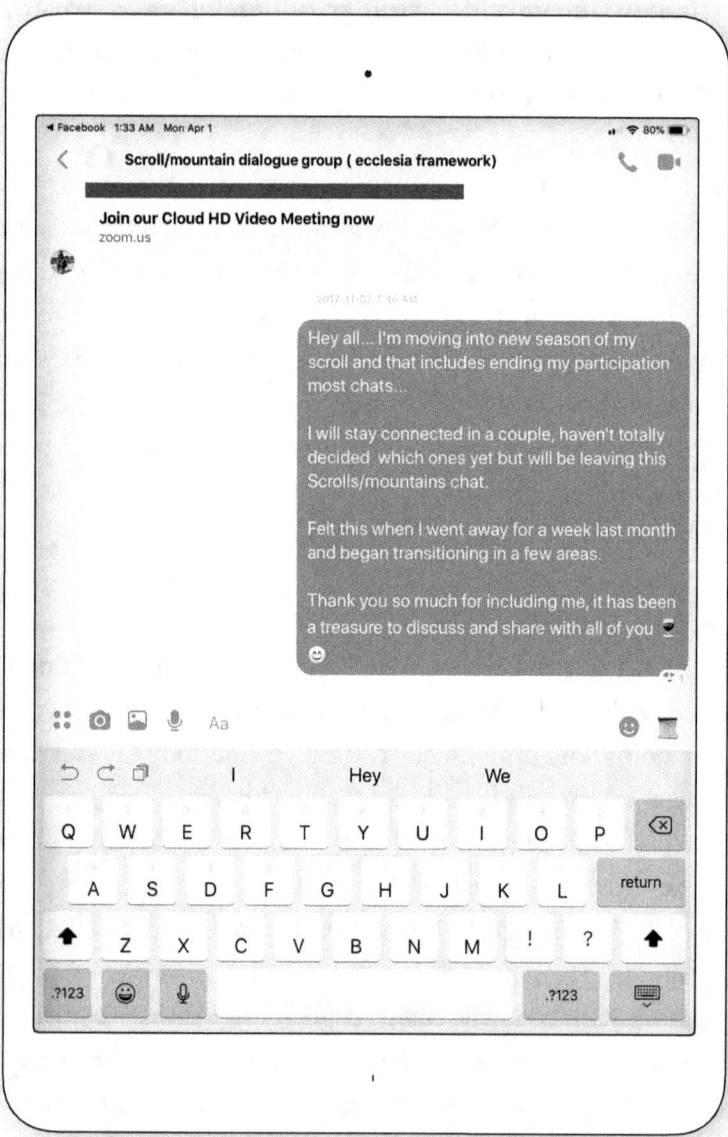

yet many with bright shiny armour were blinded by the glare of their own armour and were being easily taken out. In addition, this shiny armour (exaltation and pride) was only on their fronts so attack from behind was easy and debilitating.

This is why I find sticking close to my scroll so key. I have wanted to false start for years now. My Father wanted me to enter his rest and cease from my striving. Jesus wanted to show me how to deal with my junk, interspersed with incremental responsibility stuff.

In the Final Quest, the brown cloak of humility made us indiscernible and stopped the blinding glare of pride as an armour.

So, the door really is in the floor (as opposed to a platform) and we must sacrifice ourselves on his altar to obtain this cloak. It is so beautiful and the last shall be first.

Endnotes

All views expressed in this book are mine and we all remain powerful to choose what we believe or agree with. I am not representing One United Body or a certain set of beliefs. In fact, since this was written, my understanding has grown and changed as more is revealed. We are all in a high growth time as our Father is revealing himself and his creation more and more to us. We all need to be willing to question our own thoughts, understanding, mindsets or grids, teachings, and paradigms and bring them into alignment with Jesus who is the Truth. I appreciate the grace afforded to 'pause' this chat in time by publishing the words that were shared. Please remain powerful to choose to agree or disagree with anything I have shared.

Sheri Scott

About the Author

Sheri Scott is an author, homeschooling mom, and entrepreneur living in Calgary, Alberta, Canada, where she enjoys life with her husband, Noah, and her three teenaged children.

As a design thinker, she has been continually seeking a view of a bigger picture in the pursuit of her heavenly home, family and Father. She started Share Resources Inc., an innovation and idea company, to help facilitate the destinies of creative entrepreneurs. She is part of the creative team for the children's illustrated book series, The TRIA VIA Journals™ by Angela Thunket, also published by SHARE.
www.thetriaviajournals.com

Her desire is that everyone experience the grand adventure of understanding their destiny and journeying into our Father's house.

www.ingramcontent.com/pod-product-compliance
Lightning Source LLC
Chambersburg PA
CBHW071251070526
44583CB00017B/2419